Play Ball!

Nancy Noel Williams

 TeachingStrategies™ • **Washington D.C.**

For Teaching Strategies, Inc.
Publisher: Larry Bram
Editorial Director: Hilary Parrish Nelson
VP Curriculum and Assessment: Cate Heroman
Product Manager: Kai-leé Berke
Book Development Team: Sherrie Rudick and Jan Greenberg
Project Manager: Jo A. Wilson

For Q2AMedia
Editorial Director: Bonnie Dobkin
Editor and Curriculum Adviser: Suzanne Barchers
Program Manager: Gayatri Singh
Creative Director: Simmi Sikka
Project Manager: Santosh Vasudevan
Designers: Ritu Chopra & Shruti Aggarwal
Picture Researchers: Judy Brown & Stephanie Mills

Picture Credits
t-top b-bottom c-center l-left r-right

Cover: Ariel Skelley/Jupiter images.

Back Cover: Maria Toutoudaki/Istockphoto, Alessio Ponti/Shutterstock,
Thomas M Perkins/Shutterstock, Joe Belanger/Shutterstock, Mike Flippo/Shutterstock.

Title page: Masterfile.

Insides: Suharjoto/Shutterstock: 3, Paul B. Moore/
Shutterstock: 4, Mario Toutoudaki/Istockphoto: tl, Mike
Flippo/Shutterstock: tr, Thomas R. Perkins/Shutterstock:
cl, 5, Lucky Dragon/Fotolia: 6, Jeffrey Myers/
Photolibrary: 7, Maria Toutoudaki/Istockphoto: 8l, Jeff
Dalton/Fotolia: 8r, Masterfile: 9, Masterfile: 10, Rob
Marmion/Shutterstock: 11, Marilyn Nieves, Istockphoto:
12, Masterfile: 13, Peter Chigmaroff/123RF: 14, Amy
K Planz/Shutterstock: 15, Rob Friedman/Istockphoto:
16, Jon Patton/Istockphoto: 17, Marzanna Syncerz/
Dreamstime: 18, Photolibrary: 19, Gorilla/Shutterstock:
20, Eva Serrabassa/Istockphoto: 21, Bel Foto/Fotolia: 22,
Masterfile: 23, Ariel Skelley: 24.

Teaching Strategies, Inc.
P.O. Box 42243
Washington, DC 20015
www.TeachingStrategies.com

ISBN: 978-1-60617-122-6

Library of Congress Cataloging-in-Publication Data
Williams, Nancy Noel.
  Play ball! / Nancy Noel Williams.
    p. cm.
  ISBN 978-1-60617-122-6
  1. Ball games--Juvenile literature. 2. Balls (Sporting goods)--Juvenile literature. I. Title.
  GV861.W55 2010
  796.3--dc22
                    2009036878

CPSIA tracking label information:
RR Donnelley, Shenzhen, China
Date of Production: July 2015
Cohort: Batch 4

Printed and bound in China

6 7 8 9 10	15
Printing	Year Printed

Oh! What shall we do? Pick up a ball.
It's time for fun. Let's play, one and all!

Balls bounce high. Balls bounce low.
Up, down. Up, down. Fast or slow.

Play with a ball. Choose yellow or blue.
Some are old, and some are new.

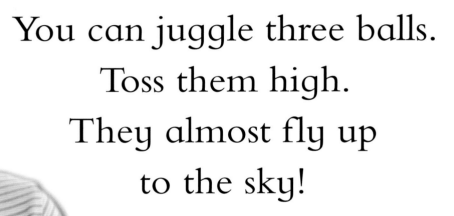

You can juggle three balls.
Toss them high.
They almost fly up
to the sky!

Oh! What shall we do? Pick up a ball.
It's time for fun. Let's play, one and all.

Throw a ball to your puppy as he runs by.
The game's called fetch. Give it a try!

Play a game of catch.
Do it right now!
Back and forth. Back and forth.
You know how.

It's your first day of practice. Go have fun.
Listen to your coach. She'll say, "Well done!"

Kick the ball low. Kick the ball high.
Soccer is exciting. Give it a try!

Play a game of T-ball. The ball sits on a tee. Swing, hit, run. It's easy. You'll see!

Oh! What shall we do? Pick up a ball.
It's time for fun. Let's play, one and all.

Draw a big circle for this game.
Try to hit a marble. Take good aim.

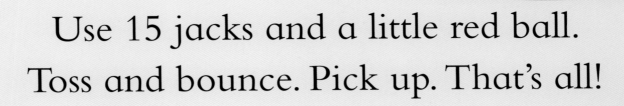

Use 15 jacks and a little red ball.
Toss and bounce. Pick up. That's all!

Put on your uniform. Grab your mitt.
You're dressed for baseball. Get a hit!

Keep your eye on the ball.
Swing right now.
Run around the bases.
You made it. Wow!

Oh! What shall we do? Pick up a ball.
It's time for fun. Let's play, one and all.

Get the ball through the hoop in basketball.
You might need a boost if you are small.

Sit on your bouncy ball. Hop, hop, hop.
Hold tight to the handles until you stop.

You can giggle and wiggle
and bop across the floor.
Up, down. Up, down.
More, more, more!

Make a touchdown. Get six points more.
The fans all cheer. Hear them roar!

Have a backyard barbeque. Go get a ball.
It's family fun for one and all!

Now it's your turn. Pick up a ball.
It's time for fun. Let's play, one and all!